The Six Trials of Jesus

And A Discussion of Modern Leadership Theories

Robert R. Thibodeau

Freedom Through Faith Ministries

PO Box 4936

Middle River, Maryland 21220

www.FTFM.org

For permissions, please contact:

Freedom Through Faith Ministries

PO Box 4936, Middle River, MD 21220

ISBN – 13:   978-0615611389

ISBN – 10:   0615611389

EBook: 9781476157726

The Six Trials of Jesus

And A Discussion of Modern Leadership Theories

All Scripture is taken from the King James Version of the Bible unless otherwise noted

Robert Thibodeau

DEDICATION

This book is dedicated to my grandchildren, Christopher, Zoe and Alyssa, who bring such joy to my life on a daily basis.

Acknowledgements

I want to thank Dr. Marc Desimone, PhD., a great friend and mentor, for his help in editing this book. His suggestions for improvement over the four years of writing this book were invaluable to the process getting it to press. I believe you will be Blessed "exceedingly and abundantly," Marc, "beyond all you can ask or think" for your contributions to this book. Thank you again, my friend.

I would also like to thank Dr. Jerry Savelle for his teachings and the opportunity to attend his Bible Institute from 1998 to 1999. I am proud to be Ordained through the Heritage of Faith Ministerial Association.

Robert Thibodeau

Table of Contents

SECTION 5:   REFERENCES AND APPENDIXES

FORWARD

By

Dr. Marc DeSimone, Sr., PhD.

What Pastor Thibodeau has done in this short work is a service to the Christian Community and those who aspire to serve in positions of leadership. I recommend this book to all men and women of good will who wish to serve others as the Master did – "He who would be first among you muse be servant of all." (Mark 9:35). I am certain you will enjoy this book.

March 19, 2012

PREFACE

This book was four years in the making. I do not say that pretentiously, but humbly. I first got the idea for this book several years ago when I heard John MacArthur deliver a sermon series on the subject of the Crucifixion of Jesus. This was before the movie "The Passion" came out. His sermon series motivated me to begin an in depth study on the Crucifixion. During the course of this study, I discovered many different aspects that are hardly ever preached upon in the pulpits of the churches I have attended.

One of those subjects was on the many trials of Jesus. The interesting thing I discovered in researching the trials of Jesus was that every single time He appeared before someone in authority during His trials – each trial was conducted illegally! As we get into this study, you will see what I mean. But the point I want to make here, is that any first year law student could have served as Jesus' attorney and obtained a "not guilty" verdict.

Then, while attending The Johns Hopkins University during my Masters Degree studies, I saw the various leadership theories evidenced in the trials of Jesus! As we were studying different Leadership theories, the Lord led me to think about how these theories of leadership were in effect, even in the days of Jesus…and resulted in the conviction of an innocent man.

Now, you may be saying, "But, Brother Bob, if that would have happened, then Jesus would not have been crucified and we would still be in our sin…." And that is absolutely true. Which is why in Chapter 21, I discuss the reasons "why" this outcome did not happen…basically, because God's Will was for it "to happen."

This book can be utilized in the classroom to give the student a perspective on the different theories of leadership as they were exhibited during the Crucifixion of Jesus as a backdrop. For those who use the contents of this book for that purpose, it is my prayer you find it informative and that it helps you in your studies.

But the primary audience for which I am writing this book is for Christians and those who want a deeper understanding of what happened during the last hours of Jesus life before the Crucifixion, with special emphasis on the trials of Jesus. Most preachers seem to focus on Jesus appearing before the Sanhedrin, and then Pilate, glossing over the other references to the actual trials he underwent in the course of 12 hours or so.

This book is not written with the intent of criticizing anyone or any particular group of people who participated in the Crucifixion. The final outcome was the Will of God. He did it in order for Him to provide the Plan of Salvation and to redeem His man back into a relationship with Himself.

When you finish reading the "Six Trials of Jesus," you will have a better understanding of various failures at all levels of political leadership in the times of Jesus. You will also be able to see these same failures in the leaders of this nation as well as companies and organizations in our society today. By paying attention to these discussions, hopefully, you will be able to identify and change the situational circumstances you encounter.

Blessed, in All You Do!

Pastor Robert Thibodeau

CHAPTER 1: HISTORICAL SETTING

In Christian theology, the single most important event that must be accepted at face value has to deal with the death, burial and resurrection of Jesus. Regardless of the denomination, if a group of people identifies itself as being Christian, then they must profess this as a Tenant of Faith. In order to get to these Tenants of Faith, we first (after the Virgin birth and living a sinless life) must arrive at the arrest and trial of Jesus. The historical facts surrounding the arrest and trial of Jesus are laden with various leadership challenges, which provide interesting parallels to challenges in today's social settings.

In this time period, Judea is under Roman occupation and subject to Roman law and authority. The Roman Caesar is Caesar Tiberius. He is a ruthless leader that has no sympathy for protestors of conquered lands. He is a provider for his subjects, but insists on absolute allegiance to Rome.

Tiberius appointed Pontius Pilate as Roman governor over the land of Judea during the times of Jesus. He is often considered the "one who killed Jesus." Although he is not actually the person who physically killed Jesus, he is the person who allowed the execution to take place. Pilate is also ruthless, sadistic and anti-Semitic.

By virtue of his position and education, he thoroughly understands Roman law and procedures and has a very working knowledge of Jewish laws and traditions. His position as governor also means he sits as Caesar's appointed judge in territorial and criminal matters. He has ultimate responsibility for enforcing Roman law and keeping peace in the territory. As he conducts his court hearings, he has developed first hand understanding of how Jewish laws under the Torah operate.

The Jewish leaders have been trying for over a year to find some reason to arrest Jesus. Jesus has consistently been a thorn in the side of the Sanhedrin Council. He has gone around the territory proclaiming the Gospel (Good News) that, basically, God is not mad anymore.

He has been teaching his followers to worship God, not the traditions which have been handed down by centuries of corrupt leaders that only want the praises of man. This message is resounding mightily throughout Judea and the Jewish leadership has decided they need to find a way to get Jesus out of their business.

Every time the Council would try to conjure up a way to arrest Jesus, he would find a way to escape. Every time they would come up with a plan to trick him In to admitting something they could turn against him, he would turn their twisted words back on them and make them look foolish in the eyes of the public.

Finally, one of Jesus' own men, Judas, came to them and offered to turn him over for a payment of 30 pieces of silver coins. He was willing to betray the One he knew and confessed (for he was a Disciple and Apostle) was the Son of God and the Messiah of Israel, for the price of a common slave.

Although Judas believed in Jesus, he never had a deep, heartfelt belief. His actions spoke louder than his words. Some believe that Judas was facing an audit of his handling of the treasury money for the disciples, and that he had misappropriated some of the money.

He knew Jesus had escaped every plan to capture him and probably believed he could gain the thirty pieces of silver he was missing by striking a deal with the elders, and then watch as Jesus escaped again. When Jesus was arrested, Judas realized what had happened and committed suicide.

Once the Jewish leadership had him in custody, they had to act quickly before the crowds could mobilize against them. Any type of riot by the people would result in a Roman crack down and, more than likely, they would lose their jobs and positions in the community.

The Jewish holiday of Passover was near. They did not want to hold unto Jesus until after the holiday, in case his followers tried to free him. They wanted to get him in front of Pontius Pilate as soon as possible for trial and to have Pilate execute him. In order to do that, they would have to prove to Pilate that Jesus had broken both Jewish and Roman laws. They knew that Pilate, though harsh, was fair in his interpretation of Roman laws.

Pilate initially did not want to even hear the case against Jesus. The Jewish leadership knew that if they brought no Roman charges there would be no Roman trial. "Without a Roman trial there could be no crucifixion. So they created charges that would cause Pilate to act or react." (Schapelhouman-de Bly, 2007). Pilate ultimately accepted the case and prepared to hold proceedings in the Roman court.

After following Roman procedures, Pilate declared there was nothing to the charges and declared Jesus innocent. The Sanhedrin protested this decision. Pilate, fearing another riot would happen, sent Jesus to Herod, a Jew in an appointed position of Roman authority over Galilee. Pilate thought he had washed his hands of this political hot potato.

Herod wanted to see Jesus, not to hear his case, but to see a magic show. He had heard about the miracles and wanted to see them performed in person. When Jesus failed to give him a show or to even respond to questioning, Herod sent Jesus back to Pilate saying he did not find guilt in Jesus either.

Pilate then presented Jesus before the Sanhedrin and the people that had gathered and proclaimed Jesus' innocence again. Now the mob was becoming truly unruly and Pilate ended up issuing the sentence of death by crucifixion to be carried out against Jesus.

As we study the different leadership theories exhibited by Pilate and the Sanhedrin, it is important to remember "Theory should be comprehensive and must be coherent, and at the same time it should also be simple. Theory must explain practice." (Hawkins, n.d.). Pilate and the Sanhedrin used various methods of implementing the different leadership theories in order to arrive at a mutually agreed to result – the crucifixion of Jesus.

SECTION ONE

MAJOR PLAYERS

CHAPTER 2: MAJOR PLAYER
JESUS

Jesus was known as Jesus of Nazareth. It was likely he was born not later than the year 4 B.C. (some accounts say 5 B.C.) which was the year of death of King Herod the Great. King Herod the Great is recorded in the Bible as ordering the killing of all children under the age of two years old in an effort to kill Jesus. His family had escaped this plan by escaping to Egypt prior to the soldiers arriving to carry out the edict.

Very little information is available concerning the childhood of Jesus. He grows up working as a carpenter in his father Joseph's shop. He has several brothers and sisters and has learned the scriptures well enough to impress the priests he meets in the Temple.

Beginning at about thirty years of age, Jesus began his ministry, which lasted approximately three years. During this time, despite his efforts to keep a low profile, his reputation spread, bringing him into the disfavor of the ruling class – the Sanhedrin.

The teachings of Jesus can be summarized into the following areas: God Loves You; You should love one another; Each person is valuable in God's eyes; God's Kingdom (the way God does things) has come to Earth and is available for you to operate in; The reality of God's coming judgment on non-believers; The reality of Heaven and hell; and God forgives those who come to Him and sincerely asks to be forgiven.

The ruling elite (the Sanhedrin) considered Jesus' claim to be the Son of Man (making Him the direct descendent of David and of Adam, to be equivalent to making the claim He was the Son of God.

This was considered blasphemy in Jewish culture and punishable by death. JesusCentral.com writes:

"Jesus' most controversial act was that he repeatedly claimed to be God, which was a direct violation of the Jewish law. Therefore the religious leaders asked the Roman government to execute him. In each of several official trials, the Romans found that he was not guilty of breaking any Roman law. Even the Jewish leaders recognized that other than Jesus' claim to be God, Jesus followed the Jewish law perfectly. Still the religious leaders, using the argument of political disfavor, persuaded Pilate, a Roman governor of the Southern province of Israel, to authorize an execution." *(JesusCentral.com, 2008).*

NOTES

CHAPTER 3: MAJOR PLAYER
PONTIUS PILATE

Pontius Pilate (born about 4 B.C. and lived until A.D. 36).was the sixth Prefect from Rome to rule over the province of Judea. He ruled from A.D. 26 to 36 and had the second longest rule of the Prefects. His family linage was the Pontii family. These were Knights which led the resistance to Roman expansion into the region of Italy known as Samnium (Lendering, n.d.). Based upon the pledge of loyalty and the fierceness with which the family clan had proven them selves in battle, freedom was granted to the family.

The name Pilate is a derivative of the Latin word Pileatus, which means a "cap or badge of a manumitted slave," meaning that he was a freedman or descendant of one. (Chrisiananswers.net, n.d.).

Judea was a land so disliked as a province, no Roman Senator wanted to go there to be the governor. This job fell to the order of knights and had the title "Prefect." In the Roman Empire, advancement was based upon patronage. Legend has it that Pilate was promoted by Syranus, the Chief Administrator for Caesar Augustus. (Encyclopedia Britannica Online, 2008).

One of Pilate's known advisors prior to going to Judea was Joseph Caiaphas, selected as High Priest in A.D. 18 by Pilate's predecessor, Valerius Gratus. Pilate relied upon the High Priests to help maintain order. (Lendering, n.d.).

Upon arrival in Judea, Pilate immediately became embroiled in controversy. He established his headquarters in Caesarea. He only traveled to Jerusalem during high feast days when he wanted to ensure no rebellion would erupt. His soldiers brought with them statues of the Emperor and placed them around Jerusalem in honor of the new Emperor Tiberius. This is in violation of Jewish traditions and was met immediately with protests.

In his efforts to be stubborn and show the Jews who was in charge, he refused to have them removed. The Jews chose the four sons of Herod the Great to intercede on their behalf. The four sons were considered equal in stature with kings by the Romans (Lendering, n.d.).

When Pilate refused to have the statues removed, Herod Antipas filed a petition directly with Caesar. Tiberius was outraged with Pilate and wrote a rebuking letter to Pilate telling him to immediately remove them and to honor the Jewish traditions.

Pilate then used money from the temple treasury to fund the completion of an aqueduct in Jerusalem. The fact that he spent money from the treasury means he had to have the cooperation of the High Priest. The riots occurred probably because he was trying to take the credit for the aqueduct instead of giving or sharing credit with the Sanhedrin Council. Pilate had ordered soldiers to quell the riot and the result was "large numbers of Jews perished, some from the blows they received and others trodden to death by their companions in the ensuing flight." (Lendering, n.d.).

When word of this got back to Caesar Tiberius, Pilate was again rebuked for using abusive force. (MacArthur, n.d.). Pilate was reminded that it was Roman policy to make alliances with the local leadership and to respect their customs and traditions.

Pilate made a temporary headquarters at Herod's old palace. He would stay there when in Jerusalem. He had shields hung on the walls of the palace bearing an inscription honoring Tiberius. The Jews protested this action and asked him to remove the shields, to which he refused. Again, the Jews sent word to Tiberius that Pilate was refusing to comply with their requests. Again, Tiberius rebuked Pilate and told him to take the shields down. (MacArther, n.d.).

Rumor was circulating that an investigation was being opened in Rome about his worthiness to continue in command. His position was a political appointment, as was the office of High Priest (the High Priest was selected by the Roman governor, in this case, Pilate.

Pilate could be replaced if Tiberius felt he was not performing his duties effectively). It was important for both Pilate and Caiaphas (as well as Annas, father-in-law of Caiaphas) to hold on to power.

No accurate details are available concerning the death of Pilate. Several myths have abounded but the most acceptable story is that Tiberius summons Pilate to Rome concerning brutality on the Samaritans during an uprising Pilate had quelled. Prior to his arrival in Rome, Tiberius dies and is succeeded by Caesar Caligula.

No records are available that indicate Pilate fell into disfavor. He had been Prefect of Judea for ten years. He was probably forced to retire. It is probable he died shortly thereafter (some accounts say he committed suicide) because in A.D. 41, he was not available to refute charges made by Jewish emissaries to Caligula. (Lendering, n.d.).

CHAPTER 4: MAJOR PLAYER
HEROD

Herod Antipas was the son of King Herod the Great. He was one of four brothers and was educated in Rome. This was a type of "honorable detention" used to guarantee his father's loyalty to Rome (Lendering, n.d.).

In the year 4BC, Caesar Augustus confirmed Herod Antipas as the tetrarch of the region of Galilee. This was a political appointment and was also a way to keep kings and royalty from conquered regions loyal to Rome and the Emperor.

Herod established a city called Tiberius in honor of the new Emperor Tiberius. It was later discovered that the city was built over an old Jewish graveyard. This upset the Jews and for many years, Jews would not enter the city. (Lendering, n.d.).

Herod had come under condemnation for taking his brothers' wife, Herodius, as his wife after a brief affair. When confronted with this by John the Baptist, he had John locked up in prison. His wife, Herodius, succeeded in having John the Baptist beheaded. Jesus compared Herod to a "fox" which was a reference to a wily, unclean animal.

Herod considered himself a Jewish leader and would often travel to Jerusalem in observance of Jewish holidays. It was for this reason he was in Jerusalem for the Passover and present for his role in the crucifixion of Jesus.

CHAPTER 5: MAJOR PLAYER
ANNAS

Annas was appointed High Priest in 6 A.D. by Quirinius, Imperial governor of Syria and held the office until 15 A.D. when he was removed by governor Gratus of Judea. During this time period, High Priests were appointed and removed from office at the whim of the governor. It was a political appointment, not a Biblical appointment as outlined in the Old Testament.

Although removed from office, he still wielded great influence. For all practical purposes, he was still High Priest in the eyes of the public, even though Caiaphas held the title during the times of Jesus. (Bible History Online, 2007).

Annas was influential in the three episodes of appealing to Caesar and getting Pilate rebuked concerning the statues, the aqueduct money and the soldier's shields in Jerusalem.

Annas was in charge of the temple treasury and money exchange. No money was exchanged without his group receiving a "cut" of the profits. When Jesus ran all of the moneychangers out of the temple, Annas vowed revenge. (MacArthur, n.d.).

CHAPTER 6: MAJOR PLAYER
JOSEPH CAIAPHAS

Caiaphas was a member of a wealthy family (established by the fact he married the daughter of the High Priest). He was part of a delegation that went to Rome to discuss fiscal matters in A.D. 17. He is possibly also one of the petitioners against Pilate when Pilate took temple treasury money to finish building the aqueducts.

Appointed by the Roman governor Gratus in A.D. 18, he retained his position of High Priest until A.D. 37. His relationship with Pilate was one of mutual cooperation because Pilate had the authority to remove him from office, but never did so.

As High Priest, he also held the office of chairman of the high court (Sanhedrin Council). He was responsible for forming the council and trying Jesus. He supervised the development of the charges against Jesus to change them from blasphemy to treason prior to reaching Pilate's court.

He was considered by many to be a pawn under the true leadership of Annas, his father-in-law. As leader of the Sanhedrin, he was responsible for upholding the laws and procedures of the Council, which he willingly violated in order to obtain a conviction. (MacFarland, n.d.).

Robert Thibodeau

CHAPTER 7: MAJOR PLAYER
THE SANHEDRIN COUNCIL

The term Sanhedrin is a Hebrew translation of the Greek word meaning, "sitting together." The Jewish nation would form a local council anywhere they had one hundred and twenty men which were heads of families in the area. The local Sanhedrin would be comprised of twenty-three selected men who sat together in judgment of both civil and criminal issues in their territory. An odd number was necessary so there would always be a majority vote in decisions. They were chosen from among the elders in the village area and acted as both judge and jury in all matters. (MacArthur, n.d.).

The Greater Sanhedrin is also known as the Sanhedrin Council. The Sanhedrin Council ruled in Jerusalem, which was the capital city and chief religious center in Israel.

The Greater Sanhedrin Council consisted of seventy or seventy-two men plus the High Priest as the chairman. This gave a total of seventy-one or seventy-three votes, allowing a majority ruling in all decisions. The Greater Sanhedrin Council consisted of twenty-four chief priests, twenty-four elders and twenty-three scribes. This council was the final court of appeal. Their power would be the equivalent today of combining the offices of the President, all nine Supreme Court Justices and all members of the Congress into one body. They wielded great power and influence in Judea. (McFarland, n.d.).

Anyone who believed a lower ruling was inappropriate could appeal a lower Sanhedrin ruling to the Greater Sanhedrin Council. To have a case approved for hearing at the Sanhedrin Council level was a good omen for someone accused and convicted of a crime. The Sanhedrin Council considered itself to be the protector of the rights of the accused. They believed it was their job to ensure no innocent person would be put to death, which would bring a curse upon the land. (MacArthur, n.d.).

To ensure each person appearing before the Sanhedrin and Greater Sanhedrin Councils would receive a fair and just trial, certain procedures were put into practice. Detailed reference is contained in Appendix 1. Summaries of the procedures are in three areas as outlined by John MacArthur in his commentary *The Illegal, Unjust Trials of Jesus* (n.d.):

1. The right to a public trial. All trials were to be conducted during the hours of daylight and open to the public. There could be no secret trials.

2. The right of self-defense. There was to be a defender – someone to speak on behalf of the accused if the accused could not or did not want to speak for himself.

3. The right to confront witnesses. A person could only be convicted on the testimony of two or three witnesses. (MacArthur, n.d.).

NOTES

SECTION TWO:

TIME LINES OF EVENTS

CHAPTER 8: TIME LINE OF EVENTS
FOR THE KEY PLAYERS

20 B.C.   Herod the Great takes control of the Priestly garments and appoints High Priests. In effect, he takes control of Judea.

12 B.C.   An edict by Augustus confirms the right of the Jews to send their shekel to the Temple.

7 B.C.   Herod executes two of his sons at the instigation of the third.

5 B.C.   John the Baptist is born

Late 5 B.C. –
to early 4 B.C.   **Jesus is born**

                 Magi traveling from the east arrive at Herod's court seeking the King of Jews.

April of 4 B.C. Herod dies just five days after executing his one of his remaining sons. Various Jewish factions revolt. Order is restored by Varus who takes command of Judea, Samaria and Galilee.

                 Rome re-establishes governance and divides Herod's kingdom among his four grandsons.

1 A.D (CE)   Jews comprise approximately one percent of the Roman Empire.

2/3 A.D.   Caesar Augustus issues a decree permitting all Jews to follow their own customs and traditions, to send money to Jerusalem and avoid civic duty that would violate the Sabbath or their conscience.

6 A.D.   Annas becomes High Priest, appointed by Quirinius.

Judea is annexed by Augustus and becomes part of the Roman province of Syria.

8 A.D.   Jesus visits the Temple at age 12.

9 A.D.   In Germany, three regiments being led by Varus are ambushed and wiped out. Varus commits suicide.

August 19, 14 A.D.   Caesar Augustus dies

Sept. 14, 14 A.D.   Tiberius becomes the Roman Emperor.

15 A.D.   Gratus becomes governor of Judea and relieves Annas as High Priest. Appoints Ishmael as High Priest.

16 A.D.   Gratus appoints Eleazar as High Priest.

17 A.D.   Gratus appoints Simon as High Priest.

Late 17 or Early 18 A.D.

Gratus installs Joseph Caiaphas as High Priest.

26 A.D.   Pontius Pilate, a knight of the Samnite clan of the Pontii, is appointed by Tiberius as governor of Judea through the efforts of Sejanus, one of his closest advisors.

27 A.D.   Jesus is baptized by John and begins his ministry.
Tiberius retires to Capri. He is saved from a landslide by Sejanus and becomes all-powerful in Roman authority.

Pilate gets into trouble with Tiberius over bringing statues of the emperor into Jerusalem.

28 A.D.   Pilate gets into trouble again for taking money to complete the Aqueducts from the Temple treasury. The Jews mount a huge protest and Pilate has many of them killed while restoring order.

Herod is upset because Pilate did not consult him about taking action in Herod's jurisdiction.

Pilate gets rebuked again for bringing shields into Jerusalem with Caesar's inscription on them, offending the Jews.

30 A.D.   Year of Jesus crucifixion (see the attached time line).

36 A.D.   Pilate is summoned to Rome by Tiberius and must answer to charges of brutality.

37 A.D.   Before arriving in Rome, Tiberius dies. Pilate is made an offer to retire by Caligula.

38 A.D.   Some report Pilate may have committed suicide in this year.

41 A.D.   Assumed Pilate is dead because he fails to respond to slandering Jewish claims of incidents occurring under his authority.

CHAPTER 9: TIME LINE OF EVENTS
FOR JESUS' LAST DAY

6:00 p.m. Thursday   Jesus conducts the Last Supper with his disciples

7:00 p.m. Thursday   Judas goes to meet with the Sanhedrin

8:00 p.m. Thursday   depart for the Garden at Gethsemane

9:00 p.m. to about

midnight Thursday   Jesus prays in the Garden

                            Judas leads the Temple Guards to the Garden to
                            arrest Jesus

1:00 a.m. Friday

 morning   Temple Guards arrive and arrest Jesus

                            Arrest is based upon a sign given by Judas (a kiss)

2:00 a.m. Friday

morning   First Trial – before Annas

3:00 a.m. Friday

morning   Second Trial - before Caiaphas the High Priest and the
                            Sanhedrin Council

5:30 a.m. to 6:00 a.m.   Third Trial – before the Sanhedrin Council to formalize
                            the charges against Jesus

6:30 a.m. to 7:00 am   First trial before Pontius Pilate

7:30 a.m. to 8:00 a.m.   Second trial before Herod

8:30 a.m. to 9:00 a.m.	Third trial before Pontius Pilate
9:00 a.m.	**Crucifixion takes place**
12 noon	Darkness covers the land
3:00 p.m.	**Jesus dies**
4:00 p.m.	Joseph of Arimathaea begs Pilate to release the body of Jesus for burial
between 5:00 p.m. and 6:00 p.m.	**Jesus is buried**
6:00 p.m. Friday	Passover begins

NOTES

Robert Thibodeau

SECTION THREE:

THE ARREST AND TRIALS OF JESUS

Robert Thibodeau

CHAPTER 10:

THE SANHEDRIN COUNCIL AS COMPARED TO THE TRAIT THEORY OF LEADERSHIP IN MODERN SOCIETY

The Sanhedrin Council was considered the protector of the rights of the accused (Swindoll, 2008). The greater Sanhedrin Council consisted of seventy one to seventy three men (an odd number to avoid a tie vote) which would hear capital offense cases. The lesser Sanhedrin, consisting of twenty-three men, could not pass judgment on capital offenses. Since the Jews were under the authority of Rome, the greater Sanhedrin was charged with hearing the cases before they could be brought to the governor for a hearing. If the greater Sanhedrin Council found a subject guilty of a capital offense, they would have to refer the case to the Roman authority (Pilate) to determine the ultimate sentence.

To get a better understanding of the power the Sanhedrin Council had in Jewish society, an equivalent parallel would be to combine the law making authority of both Houses of Congress with that of the Supreme Court of the United States, with the High Priest holding the office of President. The members were made up of the "elite" of the Jews and they took their jobs very seriously (Linder, 2002).

The Trait Theory of leadership "ascribes certain personality traits and attributes exclusively to leaders." (Wren, 1995, p. 310). Wren continues by stating in his The Leaders Companion writings that "this approach creates unrealistic expectations of potential leaders as super humans nearing perfection…" (Wren, 1995, p. 310).

This definitely describes the condition of the Sanhedrin in the days of Jesus. That is what Jesus did a lot of his preaching about - the hypocrisy of the Sanhedrin leadership as they relate to the common people.

Under the Trait Theory, the Sanhedrin considered themselves as above reproach. If they decided on a certain action, there was to be no questioning, no protesting, no disobedience from the "common folk." The interpretation of the Laws of Moses, resulting in several thousand "rules" instituted by the Sanhedrin over the years, became oppressive in nature to the common Jew.

This is not how the Trait Theory of Leadership was designed to operate. But the Trait Theory, over the course of time, results in a feeling of "exclusivity and privilege" which is not available to the common man.

The Sanhedrin Council was responsible for interpreting the writings of Moses and the Laws of God into everyday rules. Jesus had been challenging the rules the Sanhedrin had put into effect. He was, in fact, challenging their authority under the Trait Theory of Leadership.

The Sanhedrin, in trying to protect the rights of the common man from unjust prosecution, were very conservative in nature and would, in most cases, try to protect the rights of an accused from the death penalty in order to avoid the possibility of executing an innocent person and being held responsible in the eyes of God. To have a case heard in front of the Sanhedrin Council was a relief for most prisoners because they knew they would have a fair trial and not be tried on emotions only.

One of the "good" things the Sanhedrin Council did was to establish procedural rules which had to be followed concerning arrests and trials in capital cases. This helped to ensure a suspects "rights" were protected and an innocent person would not be unjustly punished or executed by mistake. Allan Watson in *The Trials of Jesus* (1995) provides information taken from the *Mishnah Tractate – Sanhedrin* (Appendix A).

The following is a summary of the rules in common English as provided by Chuck Swindoll in *The Arrest and Trials of Jesus* (2008):

If a man was arrested for a capital crime, he could never be arrested at night. It had to be in broad daylight.

If a man was arrested for a capital crime, no one cooperating in the arrest could be in any way connected to the one who is accused. No arrest for a capital crime could be made based upon information given by a follower or colleague of the accused. Because they felt if the accused was guilty so were his followers.

No Jewish trial could ever be held at night. The law stated that it must be held in the daytime. Listen to the code, which is taken from the Talmud: "The members of the court may not alertly and intelligently hear the testimony against the accused during the hours of darkness."

The members of the Jewish court, after hearing the testimony of true witnesses in a capital crime, could not immediately act and judge. They were to go home and remain alone and separate from one another for two days (at the least, one full day), thinking about the testimonies they had heard. During that time, here's what they were to do. Here's the language of the code: "Eat like food, drink like wines, sleep well. And once again return and hear the testimony of the accused."

"Then, and only then, shall you render a vote."

Even the method of voting was specified. They never took an "all in favor say I, all opposed say no" kind of vote. Their vote was supposed to be taken from the youngest to the oldest so that the youngest wouldn't be intimidated or influenced by the older votes.

No trial could be held before only one judge or member, and never without a defense attorney.

NOTES

CHAPTER 11: THE ARREST OF JESUS

The arrest of any suspect is the first step in obtaining a conviction. If the rights of the accused are violated, the arrest is invalidated and the entire trial can be compromised. In the United States, we call it protection under rights guaranteed by the Fourth Amendment to the Constitution of the United States. Suspects did not have the same constitutional guarantees in the days of Jesus that we do now. However, as previously described, the Sanhedrin Council had established procedures for protecting the rights of individuals.

The problem was, every plan they used to try and trip Jesus up had failed. Now, they had an opportunity, with the cooperation of Judas, to finally arrest Jesus. The plan they put together was illegal by Sanhedrin standards, but they saw an opportunity and took it.

The illegalities were evident from the beginning. First, it was nighttime. Every time they had tried to arrest Jesus in the daylight, he managed to escape into the crowd. This time, the streets would be empty (because it was at night) and he would be easier to spot and chase if necessary. They fully expected him to run. That is why they came out with torches and lanterns (John 18:3).

Second, they used a known accomplice in the arrest (Judas). They had paid a known associate of Jesus bribe money to help make the arrest. This is a violation of Jewish law and Sanhedrin procedures as outlined previously.

Third, they went to the Roman authorities and asked for soldiers to come and help in the arrest. In John 18:12, we see a "band" of soldiers under the authority of a captain. A captain would not be dispatched unless it involved at least 100 soldiers. A centurion would have been in charge otherwise (MacLaren, 2005). Previously, they had used only temple guards and officers, but had failed. Even though it was illegal to use Roman soldiers (according to Jewish law) in the execution of Jewish arrest warrants, they did so in this instance.

Fourth, once confronted in the Garden of Gethsemane, what the Jewish elders feared actually occurred. When Jesus announced he was the one they were searching for, the temple guards and officers went backward, with some of them falling to the ground (John 18:6-10). Probably, what happened, with the large gathering of this group and the scriptures describing Jesus actually approaching them, there was a crowded scene. When the officers in front realized Jesus was directly in front of them, they tried to move back and create some space in case there was a fight. When they attempted to do this, they tripped over some of the others behind them, and a large group started to fall like dominoes!

At this point, the Roman soldiers, thinking there was resistance, came forward and placed Jesus under arrest and bound him. This was not lawful under Jewish law, but the temple officers did not stop it, they actually assisted (MacLaren, 2005). The time was approximately 1:00 a.m.

NOTES

CHAPTER 12:   THE FIRST TRIAL OF JESUS
ANNAS AND THE VISION LEADERSHIP THEORY

The first person Jesus had to appear in front of was Annas, father-in-law to Caiaphas, the High Priest. Somewhere between 1:30 a.m. and 2:00 a.m., Jesus was taken to Annas' house. Annas had been the High Priest for seventeen years and his job now was basically the treasurer of the Temple.

He controlled the currency exchange and temple offerings. If someone needed to exchange Roman currency for Temple currency, he made sure the exchange rate favored his group. The same thing happened when someone needed a goat, sheep, cow or turtle dove for an offering. Even if the person brought his own offering, it had to pass his teams "inspection." If the animal was found to have any flaw (which they almost always did), the person could return home (often a couple days journey) or, they could purchase one of the "pre-approved" animals Annas and his group had out back. A common name we could place on his operation was a type of "Mafia."

One can almost envision a type of activity that would have the "flawed animal" traded in for a "discount" off the "clean" animal. The "flawed animal" was then taken around back, cleaned up and brought out front as a "pre-approved" animal to be sold to the next person.

Some Jews still considered Annas the true High Priest and some considered him the "vice-president" of the Sanhedrin. Either way, it was he that the arresting group brought Jesus in front of first. This is a classic example of the Vision Theory in action.

Wren describes the Vision Theory as, "the job of the leader is to imagine the future direction in which a company or country needs to go and to communicate that vision effectively to others" (Wren, 1995, p. 312). When Annas was deposed as High Priest by Tiberius and Caiaphas was instituted in his place, Annas never really gave up his authority in the eyes of many of the elite. He was still running the show.

Annas was still wielding influence. His vision for the nation of Israel was still the vision held by the Sanhedrin and espoused to the people. But, while under Roman authority, he also wanted to appease Pilate and keep the peace. Therefore, using the Vision Theory of Leadership, he would influence decisions made by Caiaphas and the Great Sanhedrin which promoted cooperation and tolerance – especially where it concerned keeping the peace.

The preaching of Jesus was challenging this authority. Annas must have challenged Pilate at one point (the reason Caiaphas was now High Priest and not him). Although he considered himself still in charge, he had to communicate his vision in such a way that the Greater Sanhedrin would still accept it.

Annas had been communicating the idea that if Jesus was not dealt with severely, made an example of, even executed if possible, the Romans were going to come and clean house. Every member of the Sanhedrin would be in jeopardy of loosing their stature, reputation and livelihood. So, when Jesus was captured, in the eyes of the arresting group, Annas was still the boss.

Why would Annas want to see Jesus at 2:00 a.m.? It has been suggested that he never forgot the time Jesus ran all the moneychangers out of the Temple. He lost a lot of money that day and probably thought in his mind, "One of these days, Jesus…" and now, he had his chance for revenge.

Jesus was brought in, hands tied behind his back, being mocked and accused by Annas without any type of representation. It was still during the hours of darkness. Annas wanted to know about Jesus' friends (so he could have them arrested, too). But Jesus refused to answer. When asked about his teachings, Jesus responds with a frank response of "ask others what I taught. I did not teach in secret. I taught openly in the Temple (author paraphrase of John 18:20-21).

After stating this, Jesus is struck by an officer (verse 22). Brutality is never permitted in Sanhedrin court proceedings. Failing to obtain a confession, Annas sends him to Caiaphas. In keeping with the Vision Theory, Annas probably instructed Caiaphas to gather as many of the Council together as possible and quickly get Jesus convicted. In order to bring calm back to the normal order of the running of the temple, they needed to get rid of Jesus. And they needed to do it quickly.

Robert Thibodeau

CHAPTER 13: THE SECOND TRIAL OF JESUS – CAIAPHAS AND THE SITUATIONAL LEADERSHIP THEORY

The second trial happened between 3:00 a.m. and 3:30 a.m. In Mark 14:53, "And they led Jesus away to the high priest: and with him were assembled all the chief priests and the elders and the scribes." This trial was also illegal because it was still dark outside and it operated as another preliminary hearing. It was also conducted at Caiaphas' house, not in the council chambers, as required.

The Situational Theory "urges leaders to focus first upon the situation and the readiness of the group to perform and work together (Wren, 1995, p. 312). Caiaphas had probably been instructed by Annas (his father-in-law, the ex-high priest), to get as many people together as quickly as possible and to try Jesus immediately and get a conviction. (Swindoll, 2008).

This time, they had witnesses come forth. The problem was, the witnesses kept contradicting each other. Caiaphas had to find a way to get this conviction and get Jesus to the Roman courts by morning. The problem he was now facing, was that his witnesses testimony disagreed with each other. Therefore, he has no basis of fact for a conviction under Jewish law (Deuteronomy 19:15). So he did something that is totally illegal according to Sanhedrin procedures – he took up the role of prosecutor and began questioning the defendant himself (Mark 14:60).

When Jesus failed to respond, he finally asked him directly, "I adjure you by the Name of Living God that you tell us if you are the Christ, the Son of God."

Any time a pious Jew heard or was asked a question phrased like that, he was obliged to answer (Swindoll, 2008). Under oath, Jesus could not plead any amendment, he had to answer!

And Jesus did answer, by replying in Mark 14:62, "And Jesus said, I am: and you shall see the Son of man sitting on the right hand of power, and coming in the clouds of Heaven."

At this point, Caiaphas stood up and ripped his garment asking, "What do we need witnesses for?" The Talmud required any time a High Priest heard blasphemous words, he was required to rip his garment. This is in violation of the teachings of Moses that stated any time a High Priest tore his garment, he was no longer in the office of High Priest (Leviticus 10:6 and 21:10). Just like politicians today, we keep some parts of the law that we like and conveniently change the ones we don't.

Now, even if this "confession" was legal, the vote for conviction did not follow legal proceedings, either. Instead, he simply asked the group present, "What do you think?" (Verse 64). And all of the Sanhedrin members present offered a mass voice vote to convict. They then gathered around Jesus and began to spit on him and beat him (also in violation of Sanhedrin procedures). Caiaphas had the group on his side. All he needed to do was to hold a daylight session to formalize the vote.

The Situational Leadership Theory was in operation. He had succeeded in his position as the High Priest and Chief of the Sanhedrin Counsel in obtaining the Guilty Verdict against Jesus. He had succeeded in convincing the majority of the members present to see his side (and Annas side) of the charges.

This is what happens if people in leadership positions begin to wield unquestionable power and are able to provide "benefits" to those whom they need support from. We can see this in operation in our own political system and corporate culture today.

But, with the Sanhedrin, we will see that even the "formal vote" would be an illegal proceeding. Actual Jewish law established by the Sanhedrin Council's procedural rulings forbid a capital offense case from receiving a verdict of guilty without at least a 24 hour (preferably a 48 hour) gap where the officials would contemplate the testimony they had heard. This did not happen in the case of Jesus. The full Council, led by Caiaphas and endorsed by Annas, had met illegally, conducted an illegal proceeding and provided an illegal verdict.

Robert Thibodeau

CHAPTER 14:   THE THIRD TRIAL OF JESUS
ANNAS, CAIAPHAS AND THE POWER THEORY OF LEADERSHIP

By this time, Jesus had been awake almost 24 hours (based upon details of His day in the Bible: traveling to Jerusalem, preparing for the Last Supper Meal, etc.). He has been beaten. He is bleeding, bruised and still bound. It is still dark outside. There has not been a trial yet which would be recognized by Roman authority.

Luke 22 records the time as approximately 6:00 a.m. Mark says it was early morning. With day break approaching, the Sanhedrin needed to act swiftly. Somewhere between 5:30 a.m. and 6:00 a.m., they would have convened in an attempt to have a "formal" trial, right at daybreak. This third trial was the shortest of the three Jewish trials.

Caiaphas knows that time is of the essence. He jumped right in as the High Priest and, acting in the role of the prosecuting attorney, took over the proceedings. Wren describes these actions in his definition of the Power Theory as "the movers and shakers who get things done...resulting in complacency or passivity among followers. (Wren, 1995, p. 312). Annas used the Power Theory in influencing Caiaphas to take action (Wren describes the use of the Power Theory by the leader, in this case Annas, to empower others – Caiaphas – as a way to increase his own power base).

By encouraging his loyal friends on the Greater Sanhedrin, Annas provides the extra validation for Caiaphas' attempts (though misguided and illegal) at holding these proceedings under "emergency" guidelines in order to gain the conviction of Jesus. Since the "power brokers" were supporting Annas and Caiaphas in this proceeding, the members in "lower standing" exhibited their passivity and just "went along."

Caiaphas led the proceedings but did not bring in the witnesses whose testimony failed the night before. Perhaps there were some members of the Greater Sanhedrin who were not present the night before. For whatever reason, Caiaphas started the proceedings by jumping immediately to the questioning of Jesus (which was not allowed under Sanhedrin procedures, the responsibility for questioning belonged only to the prosecutor).

When asked by Caiaphas if He was the Christ, Jesus replied, "If I tell you, you will not believe me. If I ask you a question, you will not answer me." Jesus was basically responding to them saying and insinuating (paraphrased), "If I answer your questions, you will not want to hear what I have to say and will not believe me. Since I have no attorney here, I then have to ask my own questions of you. If I do this, you will not answer me. So why should I waste my time responding to your questions that you are not even supposed to be asking me?" With this answer, he was bombarded by more questions from the group asking him if He was the Son of God. Jesus replied, "You say that I am." He did not answer yes or no, simply, "that is who YOU say I AM." (Author paraphrase of Luke 22:67-71).

With this response, the more influential members of the Greater Sanhedrin Council is said to have stated, "We don't need any further witnesses. We have heard this blasphemy with our own ears from his own mouth." (MacLaren, 1995). There was no blasphemy spoken. Jesus simply answered there question by stating, "That is who YOU say I am."

A vote was then taken to determine His guilt and the sentence. Remember, Sanhedrin procedures call for at least 24 hours (preferably 48 hours) between the time the testimony is finished before a vote for guilt is cast. In addition, prior to the vote being taken, the Council was to hear the testimony all over again. But not today. Not in this proceeding. Not when it concerned Jesus.

When the vote was to be taken, it was supposed to start at the youngest member of the council and proceed to the eldest. This would preclude the votes of the senior members from influencing the impartial votes of the younger members. (Watson, 1995). The Sanhedrin Council failed in this area as well.

A mass vote was initiated with a verdict of death and Jesus was led away to Pontius Pilate, the Roman Governor of Judea (Luke 23:1). Caiaphas had succeeded in getting the Council to convict Jesus. He knew blasphemy charges would not get the death sentence in front of Pilate, so on the way, he had the scribes write out the charges to give to Pilate which read:

"We find in the Sanhedrist tribunal that this man is an evildoer and a disturber of our nation in that he is guilty of:

"1. Perverting our nation and stirring up our people, teaching them to commit rebellion."

"2. Forbidding the people to pay tribute to Caesar."

"3. Calling himself the king of the Jews and teaching the founding of a new kingdom."

(Urantia Foundation, 1955).

CHAPTER 15: THE FOURTH TRIAL OF JESUS PONTIUS PILATE USING THE ORGANIZATIONAL AND VISION LEADERSHIP THEORIES

We now look at the situation in which Pontius Pilate found himself. He had been troubled with numerous uprisings in his territory by Jews who were upset with his leadership. He was under investigation by Caesar and in danger of being relieved of his command. He did not want this case dealing with Jewish superstitions and traditions. He knew that regardless of what decision he would make, somebody would be upset and the risk of another riot is something he did not want to take (MacLaren, 1995).

By way of appointment, Pilate now finds himself ultimately responsible for the Judean territory. This is an example of the Organizational Theory. Pilate was not elected nor approved by the subjects under his authority. In fact, Pilate had a complaint filed against him to Tiberius by the leaders of the Jews. One of the signers of the petition was Herod (whom he will send Jesus to for the fifth trial). Wren describes the Organizational Theory as narrowing "leadership to the position which any leader occupies in an organization" and this position "ignores the distinction between authority and leadership" (Wren, 1995, p. 311).

The way this leadership theory should work is that the leader is appointed to his position and is not selected from among those he is to supervise. This is to allow the leader the ability to make unbiased decisions in leading his organization. He is only responsible to the person who appointed him. Unfortunately, this type of position also leads to abuses of power against those under the authority of the appointed leader. The only person whom the leader is trying to impress is the appointing authority.

This answers the question of why Pilate acted in ways which infuriated the Jews concerning the statues of the Emperor he placed around town. He wanted to impress Caesar and did not care about what the Jews thought. This also explains why he spent Temple money for the aqueduct and wanted to take credit for it before Caesar. It also explains why he wanted his soldiers to carry shields with Caesar's image on them. He was trying to impress the one who appointed him.

When the Jews rebelled, he moved quickly to suppress the uprising (the Roman way). When the Jews complained to Caesar in each of these instances, Pilate found himself in trouble. The only thing he was trying to do was to impress his boss. Now, he was under review for possible replacement. He did not want any more trouble. When the Sanhedrin brought Jesus before him, Pilate sensed this was going to be trouble.

The Sanhedrin Council brings Jesus to Pilate somewhere about 6:30 a.m. to 7:00 a.m. They do not want to enter the official court area because of the coming Sabbath holiday (to do so would make them ceremoniously "unclean" and unable to eat the Passover meal). Pilate has been around Judea long enough to recognize this, so out of respect for their tradition, he comes outside to meet them. (MacLaren, 1995).

According to Roman law, there were four parts to any court proceeding. The first is Accusation, followed by Interrogation, Defense and then Verdict. Pilate asked the group what the accusations were. Instead of answering with a direct charge, the elders of the Sanhedrin responded with, "if he was not guilty, we would not be here." (Swindoll, 2008).

Pilate was not interested in hearing the case of a blasphemer. That is why he told the Council elders, "you take care of it according to your law." He did not realize he had a capital offense case before him. That is when he was told, "It is not lawful for us to put anybody to death." (John 18:31). That got Pilate's attention! He was told this was a case of treason (not the blasphemy charge to which Jesus was "convicted" of). Since Jesus was being called, the "King of the Jews" (another Caesar), the Sanhedrin figured they could convince Pilate that Jesus was a threat to Roman authority and thus be eligible for the death penalty (Lendering, n.d).

With his interest piqued, Pilate went back into the court room (judgment hall) to talk to Jesus. Pilate comes in and out several times throughout this discourse, in respect to the Jews traditions "non-defilement" of Passover. As he takes his seat, he began the second stage of Roman procedure – Interrogation. The purpose of this stage was to probe and search for evidence against the accused. He asked Jesus, "Are you the King of the Jews?" The Bible gives us the discussion between Pilate and Jesus:

> *"Are you the King of the Jews?" Jesus answered him, "Do you say this thing of yourself or did others tell you of me?" Pilate answered Him, "Am I a Jew? Your own nation and chief priests have delivered you to me. Tell me, what have you done?"*

> *To which Jesus replied, "My kingdom is not of this world. If my kingdom were of this world, then my servants would fight, so that I should not be delivered to the Jews: but my kingdom is not from here." (John 18:33-36).*

Pilate understood that if Jesus was claiming to be the king in authority, "he would have followers fighting and carrying on a revolution, taking lives, storming the temple, ruining this procedure" (Swindoll, 2008). With no others being charged in this matter, it was obvious to Pilate that Caiaphas' claim that Jesus was a king was biased. The Bible says the Jews, "handed him over because of envy." (Mark 15:10).

We also have an independent source, Flavius Josephus, who writes in his *Jewish Antiquities* 18.63-64:

> *"At this time there appeared Jesus, a wise man. For he was a doer of startling deeds, a teacher of the people who receive the truth with pleasure. And he gained a following both among many Jews and among many of Greek origin. And when Pilate, because of an accusation made by the leading men among us, condemned him to the cross, those who had loved him previously did not cease to do so. And up until this very day the tribe of Christians, named after him, has not died out. (Lenderin, n.d.)."*

Pilate then entered the Defense stage of the trial. With no defense lawyer present to represent Jesus, Pilate assumed the role himself. He attempted to look at the case from the viewpoint of Jesus. He asked Jesus in John 18:37,

> *"Are you a king?" Jesus answered, "You say that I am a king. To this end, I was born and for this cause I came into the world, that I should bear witness to the truth. Everyone that is of the truth hears my voice."*

Pilate responds with the now famous quote, *"What is truth?"* He believed that Jesus was, perhaps mildly "besides himself," (just as some of Jesus relatives had in Mark 3:21). If Jesus wanted to be a king of some future place or some other jurisdiction that he had in his mind, it certainly was not going to bother Pilate.

At this point, Pilate entered the last stage of the proceeding – Verdict. Pilate walked back outside to the Sanhedrin Council and informed them of his decision. "I find no fault in him at all." (John 18:38). NOT GUILTY on all counts. All he found was some "spiritual kingdom that will not affect or threaten Rome! Jesus is not guilty of treason!" (Swindoll, 2008).

The Council members have stirred up the crowd of supporters and at this point they started to yell out, "He stirs up the people, teaching throughout all Jewry, beginning from Galilee to this place." (Luke 23:4-5). When Pilate heard them say "Galilee," he decided to try and get out from under this pressure by sending them to Herod. Galilee was not in Pilate's jurisdiction and if Jesus was really from Galilee, he could send him to Herod (as a Jew, Herod had an obligation to be in Jerusalem at this time in observance of the Passover holiday).

Using the Vision Theory, Pilate determined to give this case to Herod. Wren says that "ideas, solutions to problems, personal meaning and goals are the purview of leaders" who use this theory. What Pilate did was convince the Sanhedrin that they should take Jesus to Herod. Since the accused was from Herod's jurisdiction, Herod should hear the case first.

Pilate definitely had an idea and solution to his problem. His goal was to "pass the buck." He was going to send this problem to Herod. He succeeded in communicating that vision to the crowd because they offered no protest to his decision to send Jesus to Herod. Herod could not impose the death penalty (Herod was a Jewish citizen placed in a position of authority by Rome). Only Pilate had the authority in Judea to authorize the death penalty. But, he figured if Jesus had done something illegal in Galilee, he would allow Herod to find him guilty and determine the sentence. That way, if something went wrong, Pilate could blame Herod.

Robert Thibodeau

CHAPTER 16:   THE FIFTH TRIAL OF JESUS
HEROD AND THE ORGANIZATIONAL LEADERSHIP THEORY

Herod was a Jewish son of King Herod the Great. He and his brothers were educated in Rome and he was made tetrarch (ruler of a quarter) of Galilee (east side of the Jordan) by his father and had it confirmed by emperor Augustus Caesar. He was disliked by the Jew's who lived in his territory. He was a signer of a petition protesting Pilate's placing of Roman shields bearing pagan inscriptions inside the Jewish temple (Lendering, n.d.). From that time until now, there was a deep hatred between Pilate and Herod (Swindoll, 2008).

It is possible that Herod perceived Pilate was giving him a peace offering when he sent Jesus to him. All he had to do was make a ruling as to guilt or innocence. It would be to his benefit to be on the good side of the governor. Herod (as well as Pilate) needed a cooperative friend in the neighborhood. The historical and Biblical accounts refer to Pilate and Herod becoming friends after this incident.

It is also plausible that Pilate had informed Herod that he had already found Jesus innocent of the charges, but that he wanted Herod's opinion also. Herod was smart and knew if Pilate had already found Jesus innocent, he had no jurisdictional authority to hear the case. Pilate was the Supreme Court in the land. He also did not have the authority to hear and decide upon capital offense cases involving the death penalty. Treason cases were especially tricky cases in which a wrong decision could cost Herod his life (MacLaren, 2005).

Herod is simply a Roman pawn in the position of leadership. This is a classic example of the Organizational Theory in operation. This Theory deals directly with the position a leader occupies in the organization, ignoring the "distinction between authority and leadership" (Wren, 1995).

Herod knows his position is appointed. He knows he has no authority in this situation to make a legal ruling. But, he has heard about Jesus and wants to see him. Jesus had referred to him as a "fox" (Luke 13:32), which was a ceremoniously unclean animal (an insult in Jewish culture – and Herod considered himself a leader of the Jews).

Herod had heard about the miracles that had been attributed to Jesus. Herod wanted to see Jesus do a miracle in his presence – he wanted to see a magic show! Jesus also knows Herod has no authority to make a ruling in this case - and refused to answer any of Herod's questions (Luke 23:9).

Both Pilate and Herod utilized the Organizational Theory in making their decisions. They were basing their decisions on "what is good for me in the eyes of the person over me." This is not how the Organizational Theory is designed to operate. It should create an atmosphere of unbiased decision making for what is best in the organization. But, when corrupted, the result is the leader becomes selfish and makes decisions on what is only in their best interest, not the best interest of the people or the organization.

After realizing Jesus was not going cooperate and provide any miracles, and hearing the baseless charges brought by the Jewish leaders, Herod grows weary of the game and packs Jesus up dressed as a King and sends him back to Pilate.

NOTES

Robert Thibodeau

CHAPTER 17: THE SIXTH TRIAL OF JESUS
PILATE AND THE SITUATIONAL LEADERSHIP THEORY

A humorous look at what Pilate might have been thinking is provided to us by David Jeremiah in his commentary on the *Crucifixion of Jesus*:

> *Now, back at the Palace, Pilate was probably eating breakfast and thinking, "whew! I'm glad that's over." Then, as he looks out the window, here comes Jesus, bound and robed as a king." The sight was probably quite impressive.*

> *There were the seventy-one Sanhedrin Council members, the Temple guards, the Roman soldiers and, by now, quite a few of the Jerusalem population. Pilate probably choked on his toast! (Jeremiah, 2002).*

Pilate resumed his seat outside (because the Jews did not want to defile themselves prior to the Passover). He wanted this over with. He had already pronounced Jesus as innocent. He had even sent them to Herod (one of their own) - and even Herod could find nothing to their charges. Pilate knew Jesus was popular with the population of Jerusalem, so he decided to include the populace in this session instead of just the Council members. He thought the voice of the people would assist him in setting Jesus free (MacLaren, 2005).

Being placed in this situation, Pilate used the Situational Theory of leadership in his efforts to use the crowd to try and release Jesus. At least, that is what Pilate was hoping would happen.

Wren describes the Situational Theory of leadership as acknowledging "that leadership necessitates varying degrees of interaction between the group and a leader." Continuing, Wren states, "This transactive view of leadership suggests that effective leaders adapt their leadership style to provide what the group needs and in return, the group "follows" the leader." (Wren, 1995).

The leader who uses the Situational Theory is trying to lead by popular consensus. He or she will "feel out" the feelings of the crowd and determine what decision is favored by the majority. A true leader will try to influence the crowds "leaders" to see things from his perspective and send these "leaders" back into the crowd to influence others of the accuracy and validity of the decision being made. A weak leader, instead of influencing the minor "leaders," ends up accepting the beliefs of the crowd and changes the plans and policies to appease the crowd.

Pilate, using the Situation Leadership Theory, attempted to inform the group that he had found Jesus innocent of the charges. He then informed them he even sent Jesus to Herod for a hearing about offenses which might have occurred in Herod's jurisdiction and Herod even had found him innocent as well (McFarland, n.d.).

The Sanhedrin Council, using the Situational Theory as well, had already planted confederates among the crowd to work them into a frenzy. It probably started as a few voices shouting "crucify Him" that caught Pilate's attention.

Pilate's wife had sent him word not to condemn Jesus because of a dream she had about Him. Pilate was also approached by some Jews (a minority who probably wanted to see Jesus released) and reminded him, that at Passover, it was customary for the governor to release a prisoner as a sign of good faith. Pilate thought this was an excellent idea. Surely this would get him out of this mess!

But, instead of just releasing Jesus, he spoke to the crowd (still trying to win crowd approval under the Situational Leadership Theory) saying, "You have a custom that I release one prisoner to you at the Passover. So, whom do you want me to release to you, Barrabas or Jesus who is called Messiah and King of the Jews?" (Matthew 27:17; John 39). Pilate believed the crowd would immediately yell out to release Jesus. He was shocked when this did not happen, but the opposite occurred – they yelled back "we want Barabbas released!"

Barabbas was the leader of an insurrection group and had been arrested for murder. He was the son of a rabbi (Bar = "son" and abbas = "father or master" – a name for a rabbi). (Konig, 2008). He had brought discredit to his father, his family and the priesthood. Pilate believed "This surely would generate support from the Sanhedrin Council as well as the people to keep this type of person locked up." Instead, he was shocked to hear the crowd yelling out, "give us Barabbas." (Luke 23:18). Pilate tried unsuccessfully three more times to appeal to the crowd and obtain Jesus' release. Each time they responded with "away with Him, crucify Him and release to us Barabbas."

Pilate then came up with a plan to appease the thirst for blood the crowd was calling for and still obtain pity for Jesus. He would have him taken inside the prison and beaten, then bring him back outside. Maybe he could appease them and appeal to their sense of compassion once Jesus was beaten. Instead of being the "Leader" and making the appropriate decision, Pilate was still trying to gain popular consensus to allow him to make the "people happy." But it was not working.

After having his soldiers beat Jesus, he brought Jesus, weakened, beaten and bloody, out to the crowd and told them, "Behold the man," meaning, "Don't you think he has suffered enough?" (Turner, n.d.). But the crowd started yelling out again, "crucify Him, crucify Him." Pilate asked them, "Why? What evil has He done. I have examined Him and found Him to be guilty of nothing."

But the crowd would not be appeased and, in fact, it began to get rowdier. The crowd yelled out, "We have a law and according to that law He must die, because He made Himself the Son of God." When Pilate heard this statement, he was more afraid than ever.

He had already been in trouble twice when the Jews appealed directly to Caesar about other god's being erected in their presence (once when the image of Caesar was brought in on standards and again with an engraving of Caesar on the shields of the soldiers). Pilate had been rebuked by the Emperor both times and did not want to have word of another false god accusation going back to Rome. (MacArthur, n.d.). He went back into the headquarters and asked Jesus, "Where are you from?" But Jesus did not give him an answer. So Pilate said to him,

> "You're not going to talk to me? Don't you know that I have the authority to release you and the authority to crucify you?"

> "You would have no authority over me at all," Jesus answered him, "if it hadn't been given you from above. This is why the one who handed me over to you has the greater sin." (John 8:11).

The Jew's were well aware that Pilate was arbitrary and cruel. But they were also aware that he was extremely sensitive to anything that would upset his standing in the eyes of the emperor. They would use this fear of upsetting the emperor to intimidate Pilate.

Pilate then made another attempt to intercede and save Jesus from crucifixion. Recalling his wife's note and remembering Greek mythology of the god's coming down to earth, he was "confused by fear, bewildered by superstition and harassed by the stubborn attitude of the mob" (Urantia Foundation, 1955). Pilate asked them, "Shall I crucify your king?" But the Jews shouted back, "If you release Him, you are not Caesar's friend. Anyone who makes Himself a king opposes Caesar!"

John MacLaren in his sermon guide *The Arrest and Trials of Jesus* writes the final explanation of what Pilate did:

> The prospect of a charge of his aiding and abetting such a crime as treason, in addition to the other charges that a guilty conscience told him might be brought against him, proved too much for the vacillating procurator. He brought Jesus out and sat down again upon the judgment seat placed upon the pavement. He made one more appeal, "Shall I crucify your King?" The chief priests gave the hypocritical answer, "We have no king - but Caesar" (MacLaren, 2005).

What did they just say? Pilate could not believe his ears! He had been trying to get the Jewish leadership to recognize Roman authority since he arrived. Every decision he had made was met with resistance. Now, here were the leaders of the Sanhedrin Council, the leaders of the community and the community at large, all gathered together and willing to proclaim their allegiance to Caesar! All he had to do was simply allow them to crucify Jesus! He could not pass up this opportunity to finally have something good to report back to Rome!

John MacArthur in his article *"Jesus Before Pilate,"* accurately suggests the Sanhedrin Council blackmailed Pilate into crucifying Jesus. When they made the statement "anyone who makes himself a king is no friend of Caesar," they were insinuating (and seriously reminding Pilate) that they would report this incident back to Rome. (MacArthur, n.d.).

Pilate then took a basin of water and washed his hands in the presence of all the people (a Jewish tradition) saying, "I am innocent of the blood of this righteous man; see ye to it." To which the Jews replied, "His blood be on us, and on our children" (Matthew 27:24, 25).

The trials of Jesus were now over. Pilate had failed at his attempt in using the Situational Leadership Theory in trying to free Jesus. In his book, *"The Leaders Companion,"* Wren writes, the Situational Theory of leadership, "measures leaders in terms of their ability to influence a group rather than to act in concert with it." (Wren, 1995). This is exactly what Pilate did – acted in concert with the mob mentality. Therefore, he failed in his attempts to use the Situational Leadership Theory in his attempts to free Jesus.

NOTES

CHAPTER 18:   THE OUTCOME OF THE TRIALS

The Jewish leadership of the Sanhedrin Council was embarrassed by the teachings of Jesus and they were afraid they losing control and influence over the general public. They knew He was called and anointed by God, as testified to by Nicodemus (a member of the Sanhedrin). What they did not want was to lose their control and power. The adage "absolute power corrupts absolutely" can definitely be identified in operation here.

During the past couple of years, they had made several attempts at tricking Jesus into admitting, confessing or claiming something which could be turned against Him by the authorities. Every time they had tried, Jesus was able to pick up on their tricks and turn their own questions back against them, embarrassing them publicly. They sent officers of the Temple to arrest Him, but they failed every time. He always got away.

Judas was in charge of the money bag and some theorize he was running a little short and possibly facing an audit. He knew the Sanhedrin would pay him to turn Jesus over and he tried to capitalize on the plan. He fully expected Jesus to get away again. When Jesus would get away, he could claim he did his part and he would keep the money. But his plan backfired wehn Jesus was arrested. When he seen Jesus was going to be taken to Pilate, he knew what he had done and could not live with himself. He committed suicide the same night.

Jesus was arrested at night – in violation of Jewish law. He was taken before Annas, who was not the High Priest, for His first trial. He was questioned, beaten and taken to Caiaphas. The second trial, before Caiaphas, was not legal either. It was held at night and conducted at his house, not the Council chambers. He did not protect any of Jesus' rights as required.

In fact, he trampled most of the specified requirements in his attempt to get a conviction. Witnesses gave testimony that did not agree; he allowed the beating of Jesus; he conducted the questioning of Jesus himself instead of listening to the prosecutor present evidence – all procedural items any first year law student would be able to use to get Jesus an acquittal on (or at least declare a mistrial). Caiaphas then conducted an "official" trial at daybreak, just to take a mass vote – which also was not allowed under Jewish law.

Jesus was then taken before Pontius Pilate. But the charges of blasphemy, of which He was "convicted" on, failed to appear. Instead, charges of treason were brought before Pilate. Pilate was told that Jesus had been found guilty of treason.

Pilate tried to give Jesus a fair trial. Indeed, he did so, and found Jesus not guilty. But when he announced his results, the Council rebelled. Fearing a protest and riot, he offered to send Jesus to Herod Antipas, a Jewish leader from Galilee who was in Jerusalem for the Passover. Herod also found Jesus not guilty and sent him back to Pilate.

Pilate tried again and again to have Jesus released. He even offered to have Jesus beaten if the crowd would let Him go (notice - he offered to have a man he found innocent to be beaten anyway). The crowd would have nothing less than Jesus crucified. Finally, after being threatened with blackmail, Pilate relented and gave the order to execute Jesus.

NOTES

CHAPTER 19:   WHAT IF....?
A LOOK AT WHAT SHOULD HAVE
HAPPENED BY THOSE WHO SHOULD HAVE INTERVENED

Alternative Outcomes Person #1: Caiaphas

The main person who could have influenced the fair treatment of Jesus, was Joseph Caiaphas, the High Priest and chairman of the General Sanhedrin Council. He was the person charged with the ultimate responsibility of ensuring the Sanhedrin conducted its affairs according to established procedures, laws and rules.

Beginning with the plan to arrest Jesus, Caiaphas could have stopped the illegal activity of planning to pay a bribe (violation of law) to a known co-conspirator of Jesus (violation of law) in an effort to have Jesus arrested at night (violation of law). He could have prohibited the use of Roman soldiers assisting the Temple guards in the ultimate arrest of Jesus (violation of law). He could have given orders that Jesus was not to be beaten or tortured prior to being convicted (violation of law).

He could have stood up to Annas, who had no right to interrogate Jesus at his house (violation of law) or to interrogate Him without the benefit of an advocate (violation of law). He could have simply told the guards to take Jesus to a holding cell and to assemble the Council at daybreak – but he did not do that. He held the trial right there at his house (violation of law) at night (violation of law).

He could have said that there were no witnesses in agreement as to their testimony concerning Jesus - and set Jesus free. But he did not do that, either. Instead, he stopped calling witnesses (when he realized they were giving contradictory testimony) and began to ask Jesus accusatory questions himself (violation of law), without having an advocate present (violation of law). Then, when he called for a vote (illegal vote at that), he simply asked for a mass voice vote (violation of law). He then allowed Jesus to be beaten and spit upon again inside the Council Chambers (violation of law).

At daybreak, he could have held an entire court proceeding, but did not do that (violation of law). He went straight into questioning Jesus himself (violation of law). When he obtained a confession (obtained in violation of law), he asked for a mass voice vote of the entire council (violation of law).

If Caiaphas would have conducted the proceedings under approved procedural rules, none of these violations would have occurred and Jesus would have been found innocent and set free. Instead, Caiaphas found Jesus guilty of blasphemy and ordered Him to be taken to Pilate.

Alternative Outcomes Person #2: Pontius Pilate

Pilate would not hear charges relating to blasphemy. Caiaphas had the charges changed to treason and insurrection (violation of law – Jesus did not even hear these charges until He was in front of Pilate).

Pilate offered Jesus a fair trial and acted responsibly when he found Him not guilty. He should have ordered the guards to let Jesus go – even taken out the back door to avoid the mob, if necessary. Instead, he keeps Jesus out in front of the mob – teasing them. As the mob starts to turn on Pilate, he offers them an alternative to go see if Herod has some charges he could find Jesus guilty of. Pilate missed this opportunity to set Jesus free.

Herod does not find anything for which he can charge Jesus with, and sends him back to Pilate, dressed (jokingly) as a king. Herod missed his opportunity to set Jesus free.

Pilate does not take the costume off of Jesus, he leaves it on and takes Jesus back out in front of the crowd. He tells them he is going to let Jesus go. Now he has really set the crowd on edge. Some of the minor leaders put into the crowd by the Sanhedrin Council begin yelling out to have Jesus crucified. Pilate takes Jesus back inside and has Him beaten (this is a violation of both Roman and Jewish law – Jesus has already been found innocent of the charges).

Pilate then brings Jesus back outside and lets the crowd look at the broken, beaten and bleeding body of Jesus. But, instead of obtaining the pity of the crowd like he expected, the crowd still wants Jesus to be crucified. Pilate missed another opportunity to let Jesus go free.

Pilate then offers to trade Jesus for Barabbas. The Jews refuse and choose Barabbas over Jesus to be set free. They insist that Jesus be crucified. Pilate missed another opportunity to exert his leadership authority and to let Jesus go.

Finally, when Pilate is threatened with blackmail by the Jewish authority (reporting this incident back to Caesar), Pilate gave in to their demands and issued the order to have Jesus crucified. He should have told the Sanhedrin that Caiaphas was fired and that he was going to make a formal report to Caesar as to why he was replacing the Chief Priest – and then replace Caiaphas on the spot for conducting illegal proceedings. Pilate knew Jesus was innocent (and had even declared Him innocent before everyone). He could have let Jesus go because Pilate knew he was in the right according to Roman law. But he failed at this opportunity also.

NOTES

Robert Thibodeau

CHAPTER 20:   THE REASON THE ALTERNATIVE OUTCOMES DID NOT HAPPEN – BECAUSE GOD'S WILL TAKES PRECEDENCE

No matter who was acting in accordance with the laws and procedures which were in operation during the six trials of Jesus, God's will had to take priority.

Without getting into a theological discussion, if God wanted to allow Jesus to face crucifixion, it was going to happen. Jesus knew this (His prayers in the Garden prior to His arrest indicate this). For further proof of this, look at the rules and procedures which the Sanhedrin had in place to ensure a fair and just trial for everyone who came before it (Appendix 1).

Look at how God moved on the leadership to ignore those procedures and to bring Jesus before Pilate. A summary of the things God had to overcome in order to get Jesus convicted are contained in Robert MacFarland's book, *Trials of Jesus*: (n.d).

> *In order to demonstrate the magnitude of the miracle that was needed to obtain a conviction of Jesus Christ, consider the errors that could have been argued by counsel:*
>
> *Illegal arrest.*
>
> *Illegal private examination of Jesus before Annas and Caiaphas.*
>
> *Defective Indictment.*
>
> *Unauthorized night proceedings of the Sanhedrin.*

Unauthorized proceedings of the Sanhedrin prior to the offering of the morning sacrifice.

The verdict based on the uncorroborated alleged confession of the defendant.

Unauthorized proceedings of the Sanhedrin on the day before a Jewish Sabbath, The first day of the feast of unleavened bread, or the eve of the Passover.

Call for a Unanimous voice verdict.

Publication of a verdict in a place forbidden by law.

Renting (tearing of) clothes by the High Priest.

Irregular balloting.

The real "theme" of Jesus' Trials is the established fact that nothing short of Divine intervention by God would have led to a conviction of Jesus. To have so many people in positions of authority, with all of the checks and balances that were in place, and have both the Roman and Jewish governing officials violate so many procedures, indicates it was the Will of God. This conviction was absolutely essential to God's plan for the redemption of man." (MacFarland, n.d,).

NOTES

CHAPTER 21:   CONCLUSION

From the proceedings we have reviewed, we can see it was God's Plan to get Jesus convicted in by the "leaders" in an illegal manner. An innocent man, convicted on drummed up charges, convicted in illegal proceedings and sentenced to death in an illegal manner – all for crimes He did not commit.

The devil was so excited about actually killing the Son of God (and thinking that would end the battle between him and God forever) – that he could actually beat God at His own plan – he never seen what was actually taking place.

The Bible actually says in First Corinthians 2:8, "Which none of the princes of this world knew: for had they known it, they would not have crucified the Lord of Glory."

If anything, Satan would have started killing "everyone" who was trying to kill Jesus! Think about that…

If the devil "knew" what was about to happen, he would have done everything in his power (limited power) to keep Jesus alive! Why would he want Jesus kept alive?   So he could have more time to "get" Jesus to commit some kind of sin (to submit to some kind of temptation) - thus nullifying the entire sacrifice. Instead, the devil fell right into the trap laid out for him before the "foundations of the world" were even set.

Satan was so "sure" his plan was going to work, he actually became the primary participant in "setting" up Jesus. You can read this account in both Luke 22:3 and John 13:27. These are the ONLY references in the Bible where it is recorded that Satan "himself" entered into and took possession and control of a person. Everywhere else it is recorded that an "evil spirit" would come on and control a person. The devil wanted to claim this "One" for himself.

So, the devil went "all in" on his gamble that this would work. Obviously, he wanted to make sure the job got done right. He had waited a long time to get to this point. He was going to thwart God's Plan once and for all. He was not going to trust this job to one of his demons. He took control of the entire situation (or so he thought).

Little did he know that in his attempt to stop the Plan of God – he actually sealed his doom and made sure the Plan of God would come to pass! Just like the Jewish leaders; just like the disciples, just like the crowds that followed Jesus – everyone (including Satan himself) – was oblivious to Jesus' actual purpose in coming to earth as a man and the suffering He was willing to go through. Including the crucifixion.

Looking back at it from our perspective, it is hard to visualize and imagine that the leaders would not have recognized Jesus for who He really was. But, they were completely in the dark – including Satan.

The Jewish leaders failed in their leadership positions. The Roman authorities failed in their leadership positions. The spirits of darkness "thought" they had fulfilled their desires and had gotten the victory….

But the only person(s) who gained the Victory on the day Jesus was crucified – was the Father, the Son and the Holy Spirit! They had planned this event from the beginning of time. They executed their plan perfectly.

There is also one more group that benefited…mankind. Believers in Jesus Christ also gained the Victory over the devil that day. Prior to His ascension, Jesus told His disciples in Matthew 28:18 that "all power is given to unto me in Heaven and in earth…" The word "power" in Hebrew means (and would have been better translated as) "authority." Jesus then goes on to delegate that authority which had been given to Him – to US! To the believers!

He then ascended to Heaven (Acts 1:9) and has sat down at the "right hand of the Father (Psalm 110:1; Mark 16:19; Acts 7:55-56). He is there right now – presiding over all things. Waiting for "us" to take the delegated authority He gave to us and to subdue and dominate all the forces of darkness that try to influence the affairs of men in the earth.

(For further study along this line, I highly recommend you do a study of "The Blessing." This discussion is not conducive to the subject of this book, therefore I will just recommend you continue your studies in this area).

You may ask, "What type of Leadership Theory did God use to accomplish His Plan?" The answer is quite obvious (if you just think about it for a moment)…."

The Answer: HE USED ALL OF THEM!

They all are part of His being. He is the Creator of "all things." This means He fully encompasses all attributes – including the "perfect" Leadership abilities to run the entire Universe – not just mankind. God used the Theories we have discussed as follows:

Trait Theory - "ascribes certain personality traits and attributes exclusively to leaders." (Wren, 1995, p. 310). God retained exclusive control over the Plan (when it was to implemented; how it was to be carried out; who was going to be let in on the plan and what role each person would play, etc.).

The Roman and Jewish leaders took their leadership positions and used their positions for personal gain. In an attempt to hold on to their positions, they had to execute an innocent man.

Vision Theory – "The job of the leader is to imagine the future direction in which a company or country needs to go and to communicate that vision effectively to others" (Wren, 1995, p. 312). God had "imagined" the Plan from before the foundation of the world and moved events in that direction. He continued to provide insights by His Prophets throughout history to bring everything into perfect alignment for Jesus to come on the scene. God's Vision was for "all men to be saved and come to the knowledge of truth..." (1 Timothy 2:4). God had the ultimate Vision for the Plan of Salvation and communicated that Vision through His Word, and to the ultimate fulfillment of His Plan, to Jesus.

The Jewish leadership believed if they did not rid themselves of Jesus, the people would stop listening to them; stop honoring them; and possibly begin to rebel. Then the Romans (they believed) would come in and either have them executed or (in their fears) replaced! They would lose their prestige, their honor and their livelihood. That is why Caiaphas even prophesied that it *"expedient for us that one man should die for the people, and that the whole nation perish not."* This vision was effectively communicated and received by the entire Sanhedrin Council.

The Situational Theory – "Urges leaders to focus first upon the situation and the readiness of the group to perform and work together (Wren, 1995, p. 312). God used the current political and personal situations of the main players and coordinated their efforts to fulfill the plan. For "the king's heart is in the hand of the LORD, as rivers of water: He turneth it whithersoever He wills." (Proverbs 21:1). God used the weaknesses of the leadership to blind them to the true situation they were facing – the long awaited Messiah was standing in front of them. He used their pride, their greed and their fears to have Jesus offered as the sacrifice for all mankind. This fulfilled the Situational Theory that Jesus found Himself in.

The major players looked at the situation purely from the view of Roman oppression. They were in fear that the Roman governor would remove them from their offices and they would lose their authority. They were willing to do away with Jesus in it would restore the "status quo" to their lives. The Situational Theory should be used to motivate a group to perform actions in overcoming obstacles. In this instance, they abused the power of the Situational Theory by not focusing on the rules and procedures to keep order. Rather, they focused and used the Theory in an attempt to keep "their status."

The Power Theory - God used "the movers and shakers who get things done…resulting in complacency or passivity among followers." (Wren, 1995, p. 312). The passivity of Caiaphas to stand up to his father-in-law, Annas. The complacency of the entire Sanhedrin Council; Herod, Pilate, etc., all fulfilled God's Plan. God used the leadership to carry out His Plan of Salvation – even though they did not know it. Just as Pilate was corrected by Jesus when He said, "You could have no power (authority) over me at all, unless it has been given to you from above…" (John 8:11).

Annas and Caiaphas used their power to abolish the rules of law in the case of Jesus. They convinced the Greater Sanhedrin Council to go along with their plan. They then ended up blackmailing Pilate (causing him to become complacent in resisting their will) and receiving what they wanted – the death of Jesus.

The Organizational Theory – Wren defined this as narrowing "leadership to the position which any leader occupies in an organization" and this position "ignores the distinction between authority and leadership" (Wren, 1995, p. 311). God used the individuals who were in various positions of authority to collectively operate according to His Plan. He moved events for centuries to culminate in this day – the day of Crucifixion for Jesus.

The rulers in place that day believed they were acting in the capacity afforded to them by their position. From Caiaphas and Annas to the Sanhedrin to Pilate and Herod, each of them believed they were in a position of dominance. Little did they know that the God of the Universe had pre-ordained their participation in the greatest coup of all time.

Only God Himself could operate all of these various Theories of Leadership perfectly. Man's attempt to "label" them is just that – attempts. Only God knows the actual – the TRUE – "theories of leadership" which He has pre-ordained to be used by man.

The focus of this book has been to introduce you to the events surrounding Jesus' last day on this earth as a human being. My efforts were to explain the processes that appeared to be working against Him. These efforts appeared, on the surface, to succeed. It appeared the devil had, indeed, defeated the Son of God (and thusly, God Himself).

"But God" (one of my favorite quotes from the Bible, contained in Ephesians 2:4, among others)…had a plan that trumped the plan of the devil.

I want to leave you with this thought taken from Ephesians 2:1-8:

> *"And you has he quickened (made alive), (you) who were dead in trespasses and sins; (you) wherein times past you walked according to the prince of the power of the air (the devil), the spirit that now works in the children of disobedience: among whom also we all have had our conversations in times past; in the lusts of our flesh, in fulfilling the desires of the flesh and the desires of the mind; and were, by nature, the children of wrath, even as others (are now). BUT GOD, who is rich in mercy, for his great love wherewith he loved us, even when we were dead in (our) sins, has quickened us (made us alive) together with Christ (Jesus), (for by grace you are saved); And he has raised us up together (with Jesus) to sit together in heavenly place in Christ Jesus: so that in the ages to come, he might show the exceeding riches of his grace, in his kindness, towards us through Christ Jesus. For by grace you are saved – through Faith; and not faith in yourselves: (this faith – in Jesus) is THE GIFT OF GOD. (emphasis and additions are my attempts to "clarify" the text of scripture for you a little more clearly).*

If you are a student and studying the Theories of Modern Leadership, I hope and pray you could "see" the theories outlined in this book. I hope this discussion will help you in your further studies and in your future careers – wherever that may be.

If you are a student of the Bible and studying the Crucifixion of Jesus, I hope and pray this discussion has given you insight into all of the "drama" that was occurring around the most important event in Christian (and human) history. May it spur you on to further studies about Jesus Christ and may it assist you in reaching the lost for Christ.

If you are a leader in ministry, I pray you study these Theories of Leadership; study the events that corrupted the intended use of the Theories; and strive to implement them the way they were designed to work. Keep envy, strife and popular opinion out of your leadership decisions. Make your decisions based upon the Word of God and what the Word has to say about your situation. Make your decisions only after seeking God's Will through His Word and spending time in Prayer.

Finally, I close this book with a phrase that I use in the close of all my ministry letters, my meetings and my broadcasts. I sincerely pray this for you also:

BE BLESSED IN ALL YOU DO!

Pastor Robert Thibodeau

Freedom Through Faith Ministries

NOTES

REFERENCES

1. *Apologetics Study Bible*, (2007). Nashville, TN: Holman Bible Publishers

A night of trials, (n.d.). Retrieved March 6, 2008 from
http://www.welcometohosanna.com/LIFE_OF_JESUS/holyweek6.htm

2. Bible History Online, (2007). Annas. Retrieved March 10, 2008 from
http://www.bible-history.com/HighPriests/NTHIGHPRIESTSAnnas.htm

3. Cline, A. (n.d.). *Pontius Pilate: Profile & biography of Pontius Pilate Roman Prefect.* Retrieved March 6, 2008 from
http://atheism.about.com/od/biblepeoplenewtestament/p/PontiusPilate.htm

4. Hawkins, C. (n.d.). *Toward a theory of military leadership.* Retrieved March 9, 2008 from http://www.militaryconflict.org/leader.htm

5. Jesuscentral.com (n.d). *Brief life summary.* Retrieved March 9, 2008 from
http://www.jesuscentral.com/ji/historical-jesus/jesus-life.php

6. Konig, G. (2008). *Barabbas.* Retrieved March 10, 2008 from
http://www.aboutbibleprophecy.com/p113.htm

7. Lendering, J. (n.d.). *Caiaphas.* Retrieved March 4, 2008 from
http://www.livius.org/caa-can/caiaphas/caiaphas.htm

8. Lendering, J. (n.d). *Herod Antipas – The house of Herod Antipas.* Retrieved March 8, 2008 from http://www.livius.org/he-hg/herodians/herod_antipas.html

9. Lendering. J. (n.d.). *Pontius Pilate.* Retrieved March 4, 2008 from
http://www.livius.org/pi-pm/pilate/pilate01.htm

10. Linder, D. (2002). *The trials of Jesus.* Retrieved March 5, 2008 from
http://www.law.umkc.edu/faculty/projects/ftrials/jesus/jesus.html

11. MacArthur, J. (n.d.). Jesus before Pilate. Retrieved March 3, 2008 from http://www.biblebb.com/files/MAC/sg1572.htm

12. MacArther, J. (n.d.) *The illegal, unjust trials of Jesus – Part 1.* Retrieved February 27, 2008 from http://www.biblebb.com/files/mac/sg2389.htm

13. MacArthur, J. (n.d.). *What shall I do with Jesus – Part 2.* Retrieved March 3, 2008 from http://www.biblebb.com/files/MAC/sg2394.htm

14. MacLaren, J. (2005-2008). *The arrest and trials of Jesus Christ.* Retrieved February 25, 2008 from http://net.bible.org/dictionary.php?word=JESUS%20CHRIST,%20THE%20ARREST%20AND%20TRIAL%20OF

15. McFarland, R., Sr. (n.d.) *The Jesus Trials.* Retrieved March 5, 2008 from http://www.mcfarlandmcfarland.com/JesusTrials.html

16. McFarland, R., Sr. (n.d.). The Sanhedrin. Retrieved March 5, 2008 from http://www.law.umkc.edu/faculty/projects/ftrials/jesus/sanhedrin.html

17. *Pontius Pilate.* (n.d.). Christian Answers Network web site (Gilbert, AZ: Eden Communications, 1996). Used by permission. Retrieved March 11, 2008 from http://www.christiananswers.net/dictionary/pilatepontius.html

18. *Pontius Pilate* (2006). Encyclopædia Britannica. Retrieved March 12, 2008 from http://www.britannica.com/eb/article-9060010/Pontius-Pilate

19. Schapelhouman-de Bly, H., (2007, April6). *The Pilate error?* Retrieved March 11, 2008 from http://www.sempervita.org/leadership/

20. Swindoll, C. (n.d.). *The arrest and trials of Jesus.* Retrieved March 2, 2008 from http://ecclesia.org/truth/trial-jesus.html

21. Thomas, L. (1997-2008). *The Thomas pages: Herod to Pilate.* Retrieved March 3, 2008 from http://www.lloydthomas.org/1-IsraelTimeLine/3-ManassehHadrian/36bc-36ad.htm

22. Turner, J. (n.d.). *The six trials of Jesus.* Retrieved February 27, 2008 from http://www.turner-bible-lessons.com/files/The_Six_Trials_Of_Jesus.htm

23. Urantia Organization (1955). The trial before Pilate. In *The Urantia book* (Paper 185). Retrieved March 13, 2008 from http://www.urantia.org/papers/paper185.html

24. Watson. A. (1995) *Trials of Jesus.* Retrieved March 5, 2008 from http://www.law.umkc.edu/faculty/projects/ftrials/jesus/sanhedrin.html

25. Wren, J.T. (1995). *Leaders companion: Insights on leadership through the ages* New York: The Free Press

APPENDIX 1:

MISHNAH TRACTATE, SANHEDRIN

Verdicts in Capital Trials Only to be Reached in Daytime

[Under the Mishnah Tractate, Sanhedrin]

Mishnah Sanhedrin 4.1 In noncapital cases they hold trial during the daytime and the verdict may be reached during the night; in capital cases they hold the trial during the daytime and the verdict must also be reached during the daytime. In noncapital cases the verdict, whether of acquittal or of conviction, may be reached the same day; in capital cases a verdict of acquittal may be reached on the same day, but a verdict of conviction not until the following day.

Requirements for Conviction

Mishnah Sanhedrin 5.1-4

5.1 They used to prove witnesses with seven inquiries: In what week of years? In what year? In what month? On what day? In what hour? In what place?

(R. Jose says: [They asked only,] On what day? In what hour? In what place?)

[They also asked:] Do you recognize him? Did you warn him?

If a man committed idolatry [they asked the witnesses], What did he worship? and, How did he worship it?

2. The more a judge tests the evidence the more he is deserving of praise: Ben Zakkai once tested the evidence even to inquiring about the stalks of figs. Wherein do the inquiries differ from the cross-examination? If to the inquiries one [of the two witnesses] answered, "I do not know," their evidence becomes invalid; but if to the cross-examination one answered, "We do not know," their evidence remains valid. Yet if they contradict one another, whether during the inquiries or the cross-examination, their evidence becomes invalid.

3. If one said, "On the second of the month," and the other said, "On the third," their evidence remains valid since one may have known the month was intercalated and the other did not know the month was intercalated; but if one said, "On the third," and the other said, "On the fifth," their evidence becomes invalid. If one said, "At the second hour," and the other said, "At the third," their evidence remains valid; but if one said, "At the third hour," and the other said, "At the fifth," their evidence becomes invalid. R. Judah says: It remains valid; but if one said, "At the fifth hour," and the other said, "At the seventh," their evidence becomes invalid since at the fifth hour the sun in in the east and at the seventh it is in the west.

4. They afterward brought in the second witness and proved him. If their words were found to agree together they begin [to examine the evidence] in favor of acquittal. If one witness said, "I have somewhat to argue in favor of his acquittal," or if one of the disciples said, "I have somewhat to argue in favor of his acquittal," they bring him up and set him among them and he does not come down from thence the whole day. If there is any substance in his words they listen to him. Even if the accused said, "I have somewhat

to argue in favor of my acquittal," they listen to him, provided there is any substance to his words.

Postponement of Final Sentence Until the Day After Trial Under the Mishnah

Mishnah Sanhedrin 5.5

If they found him innocent they set him free; otherwise they leave his sentence over until the morrow. [In the meantime] they went together in pairs, they ate a little (but they used to drink no wine the whole day), and they discussed the matter all night, and early on the morrow they came to the court. He that favored acquittal says: "I declared him innocent and I still declare him innocent"; and he that favored conviction says, "I declared him guilty and I still declare him guilty." He that favored conviction may now acquit, but he that had favored acquittal [the day before] may not retract and favor conviction."

Capital Punishment By Stoning

Mishnah Sanhedrin 6.1-4

1.   When sentence has been passed, they take him forth to stone him. The place of stoning was outside the court, as it is written, Bring forth him that hath cursed without the camp. One stands at the door of the court with a towel in his hand, and another, mounted on a horse, far away from him [but where he is able] to see him. If one [in court] said, "I have somewhat to argue in favor of his acquittal," that man waves the towel and the horse runs and stops him [the stoner]. Even if he himself said, "I have somewhat to argue in favor of my acquittal," they must bring him back, be it four times or five, provided that there is any substance in his words. If they found him

innocent, they set him free; otherwise he goes forth to be stoned. A herald goes out before him [announcing], "Such-a-one, the son of such-a-one, is going forth to be stoned for that he committed such or such an offense. Such-a-one and such-a-one are witnesses against him. If any man knoweth anything in favor of his acquittal, come let him plead it."

2. When he was about ten cubits from the place of stoning they used to say to him, "Make your confession," for such is the way of them that have been condemned to death to make confession, for every one that makes his confession has a share in the world to come. For so we have found it with Achan. Joshua said to him, My son, give, I pray thee, glory to the Lord, the God of Israel, and make confession unto him, and tell me now what you have done; hide it not from me. And Achan answered Joshua and said, Of a truth I have sinned against the Lord, the God of Israel, and thus and thus have I done. Whence do we learn that his confession made atonement for him? It is written, And Joshua said, Why have you troubled us? The Lord shall trouble thee this day--this day you shall be troubled, but in the world to come you shall not be troubled. If he knows not how to make his confession they say to him, "Say, May my death be an atonement for all my sins." R. Judah says: If he knew that he was condemned because of false testimony he should say, "Let my death be an atonement for all my sins excepting this sin." They said to him: If so, every one would speak after this fashion to show his innocence."

3. When he was four cubits from the place of stoning, they stripped off his clothes. A man is kept covered in front and a woman both in front and behind. So R. Judah. But the Sages say: a man is stoned naked but a woman is not stoned naked.

4. The place of stoning was twice the height of a man. One of the witnesses knocked him down on his loins; if he turned over on his heart the witness turned him over again on his loins. If he straightaway died that sufficed; but if not, the second took the stone and dropped it on his heart. If he straightaway died, that sufficed; but if not, he was stoned by all Israel, for it is written, The hand of the witnesses shall be first upon him to put him to death and afterward all the hand of all the people. All that have been stoned must be hanged. (So R. Eliezer). But the Sages say: None is hanged save the blasphemer and the idolater. A man is hanged with his face to the people and a woman with her face to the gallows. (So R. Eliezer.)

But the Sages say: A man is hanged but a woman is not hanged. R. Eliezer said to them: Did not Simeon ben Shetah hang women in Ashkelon? They answered: He hanged eighty women, whereas two ought not to be judged in one day. How did they hang a man? They put a beam into the ground and a piece of wood jutted from it. The two hands were brought together and it was hanged. R. Jose days: The beam was made to lean against a wall and one hanged the corpse thereon as butchers do. And they let it down at once: if it remained there overnight a negative command is thereby transgressed, for it is written, His body shall not remain all night upon the tree, but thou shall surely bury him the same day; for he that is hanged is a curse against God; as if to say, Why was this one hanged? Because he blessed the Name, and the Name of Heaven was found profaned.

[Other forms of capital punishment under Jewish law included burning, decapitation, and strangulation, each of which has its own set of crimes meriting such punishment.]

Crimes Meriting Stoning

Mishnah 7.4 These are they that are to be stoned: he that has connection with his mother, his father's wife, his daughter-in-law, a male, or a beast, and the woman that suffers connection with a beast, and the blasphemer and the idolater, and he that offers any of his seed to Molech, and he that has a familiar spirit and a soothsayer, and he that profanes the Sabbath, and he that curses his father or his mother, and he that has a connection with a girl that is betrothed, and he that beguiles [others to commit idolatry], and he that leads [a whole town] astray, and the sorcerer and a stubborn and rebellious son.

Information for this appendix was obtained from the following reference.

Watson. A. (1995) *Trials of Jesus.*
Retrieved March 5, 2008 from
http://www.law.umkc.edu/faculty/projects/ftrials/jesus/sanhedrin.html

NOTES

APPENDIX 2:

MAP OF JERUSALEM ON JESUS' LAST DAY

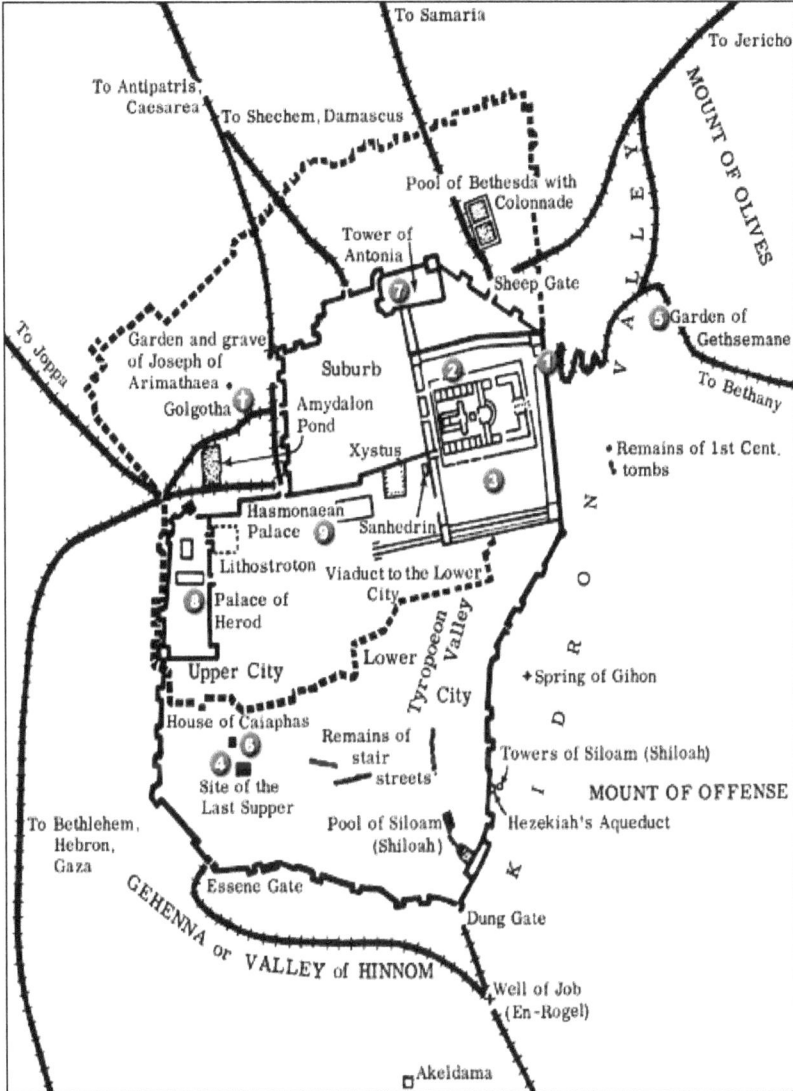

PRAYER OF SALVATION

If you have never received or made Jesus your Lord and Savior; If you have never asked Him to forgive you of ALL your sins (everything you have ever done wrong in your life; even the inherited sins of iniquity that are part of your human DNA that you had nothing to do with)…I would like you to say this prayer out loud and believe it with all your heart…because this is all that is required for you to receive the forgiveness of your sins and the FREE gift of Eternal Life:

"Father, I come to you in the Name of Jesus. I believe you sent Jesus into this earth to live a sinless life and then die a sinners death on the Cross. He did this for me. He did this for anyone who will just believe that He did it…

I ask you to forgive me of my sins. Lord Jesus, I accept your sacrifice in my place. I believe you were raised from the dead by the Power of God. I believe you ascended up into Heaven and you sit at the Right Hand of God, the Father. I believe you are coming again to take all the believers to Heaven to be with you and the Father – forever.

I thank you, Jesus, for the forgiveness of ALL my sins. I thank you for the promise of everlasting Life with you and the Father, forever. I now ask you to come into my heart. I ask you to send your Holy Spirit into my life. I ask you to lead me, to guide me and to direct my paths through this life. I am your and you are mine.

In Jesus Name I pray this prayer….**AMEN!**

CONGRATULATIONS!!!   Welcome to the Family of God!!!

You are now a Born Again Believer in the Name of Jesus!!! If anybody ever asks – you can say YES! I AM SAVED!!!

Romans 10:9-10 and 13 states "If you will confess with your mouth and believe with your heart that God raised Jesus from the dead, you shall be saved…For with the heart man believes unto righteousness and with the mouth, confession is made unto salvation. For whosoever calls upon the Name of the Lord shall be saved!"

If you prayed that prayer, will you contact us and let us know? We want to rejoice with you over the greatest gift you could ever receive – Forgiveness of sins and Eternal Life!

Just go to our website at www.FTFM.org and click on the "contact us" link and send us an email.

BE BLESSED IN ALL YOU DO!

ABOUT THE AUTHOR

Evangelist, Pastor and Teacher –

Robert Thibodeau

Freedom Through Faith Ministries (FTFM) has been proclaiming and teaching the Word of God since 1999 when Robert R. Thibodeau (Brother Bob) founded the ministry in Fort Worth, Texas. He is the founder and current director of the ministry, which has been located in Baltimore, Maryland since 2001.

Since the inception of FTFM, Brother Bob has worked with other ministries in the conduct of crusades and large-scale concerts all across America. He has seen healings and miracles take place during these events, and has realized what the Power of God can do in a persons life - once they accept Jesus as Lord! With Faith in God, all things are possible to him who believes!

The primary purpose of FTFM is to evangelize, disciple, teach and empower people everywhere to impact their world with the Gospel of Jesus Christ. "Brother Bob" does this by introducing them to Jesus as their Savior and motivating them to apply Biblical Principles in their everyday life.

In addition to his weekly radio broadcasts on selected radio stations located in various parts of the United States, Brother Bob has a weekly Internet radio broadcast, which is heard around the world.

Brother Bob has also founded the Internet radio station – "Freedom Through Faith Christian Radio" (www.FTFChristianradio.com). Beginning in October 2011, FTFCR has quickly grown into one of highest rated online radio stations in the world!

FTFCR is currently listened to on a regular basis in over 16 different countries and almost every state in the United States. FTFCR varies the programming schedule throughout the day, alternating between Praise and Worship and good, sound Bible based teaching by some of the most prestigious Bible teachers in the United States.

The focus of the radio station is to allow ministries of all types and sizes to enter the broadcast ministry market. FTFCR has several smaller ministries conducting Bible teaching to people groups all over the world – at very affordable rates.

As always, we pray for our Partners on a daily basis. YOU are the most important aspect of this Ministry. YOU are the reason we share the Gospel of Jesus Christ and what He did for us on the Cross. YOU are the reason JESUS IS LORD!

Remember, "Be of Good cheer, for Jesus has overcome the world (and all the problems of the world). And this is the Victory that overcomes the world" - your Faith and our Faith in agreement together!

For more information on Robert Thibodeau and Freedom Through Faith Ministries, or to invite Brother Bob to speak at your church or event, please visit our website at **www.FTFM.org.**

For more information on Freedom Through Faith Christian Radio, including how to broadcast on the station with your own programming, please visit our website at **www.FTFChristianradio.com**.

FREEDOM THROUGH FAITH MINISTRIES

PO BOX 4936

MIDDLE RIVER, MARYLAND 21220

UNITED STATES OF AMERICA

Other Books Currently in Print

by Pastor Robert Thibodeau

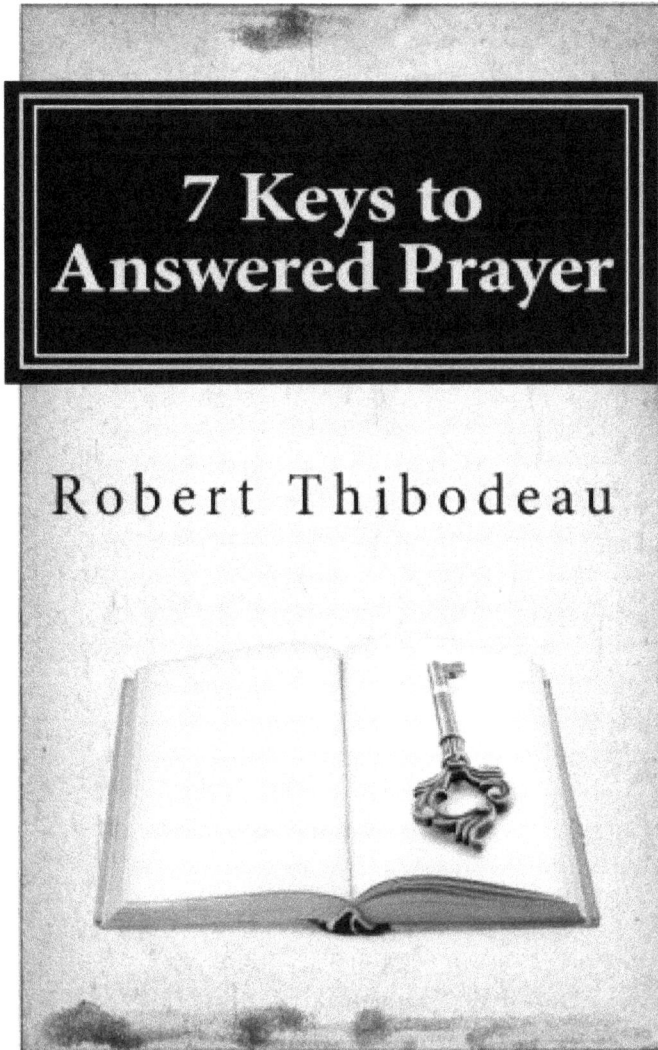

Have you been wondering why your prayers are not being answered? This book by Pastor Thibodeau will help you to find the "Keys" to receiving from God. $12.95 at Amazon.com, Barnes and Noble and other online retailers. E-Version is also available.

Another book, intended for Licensed and Ordained Ministers and Pastors. It makes a great gift!

The Marriage Ceremony

A Step by Step Guide for
Pastors and Ministers

Robert Thibodeau

This handbook is a ready reference for conducting any marriage ceremony. Step by step instructions and verbatim guides allow you to conduct Traditional, Civil and Episcopalian style wedding ceremonies. This is the actual handbook Pastor Thibodeau has been using for almost twenty years in his wedding ceremonies! Now available for $7.95 on Amazon.com and Barnes and Noble websites.

These books are available in print format and electronic format on Barnes and Noble and Amazon.com as well as through our website: www.FTFM.org

Be Blessed In All You Do!

Robert Thibodeau

www.ingramcontent.com/pod-product-compliance
Lightning Source LLC
LaVergne TN
LVHW061224060426
835509LV00012B/1413